How to Start, Run, and Grow a

Non-Emergency Medical Transportation Business

A Step-By-Step Startup Guide to Starting a Successful NEMT Business

By

Matt Bower

Copyright © 2020 – **CSBA Publishing House**

Email:csbapublishing@gmail.com

All Rights Reserved.

No part of this publication may be reproduced, stored in a retrieval system or transmitted in any form or by any means, electronic, mechanical, photocopying, recording or otherwise without the proper written consent of the copyright holder, except brief quotations used in a review.

Published by:

CSBA Publishing House
Cover & Interior designed

By

Jackie Sanford

First Edition

Contents

Personal Thanks 7

What is Non-Emergency Medical Transportation (NEMT)? 8

    NEMT Defined 9

    Other NEMT Solutions 10

    How NEMT Works 12

        NEMT Broker 13

        NEMT Fleet 14

The History of NEMT 16

The Evolution of NEMT 21

    Increased Awareness of the Need for NEMT Services 23

    Moving Care Beyond Traditional Settings 24

    The State of the NEMT Industry 27

        Cost Reductions 29

        Changes in Healthcare Transportation 30

Brand and Customer Awareness 32

    Location 33

    Types of Transportation 35

    Gauge Your Experience 38

    A Great Start 41

Writing a Business Plan for Your NEMT Business .45

Why You Should Have a Business Plan 47
- Action Plan 47
- Generating New Ideas 48
- Reality Check 49
- Decision Making 50
- It's a Necessity 50

Parts of a Business Plan 51
- Executive Summary 52
- Company Description 56
- Operating Expenses 58
- Market Analysis 59
- Competitive Analysis 61
- Projected Loss and Income Statements 63
- Promotional and Marketing Plan 64
- Operations and Management 67
- Market Potential and Target Market 70
- Financial Statements 71
- Request for Funding 72

More Help with Writing a Business Plan 74

Long-Term Success 75

Business Structure and Finances 77

Sole Proprietor 78

Partnership 78
- General Partnership 79
- Limited Partnership 79
- Joint Venture 80

Limited Liability Corporation (LLC) 80

Corporation 82

Obtain an EIN 82

Business License and Articles of Incorporation........... 83

Business Bank Account 84

Obtain Financing 85

Start-Up Costs 86

Insurance 88

How to Run Your Business *95*

Create a Company Handbook 97

Create Job Descriptions 99

Customer Service 100

Happy Customers.. 101

Handle Complaints Well 106

How to Grow Your Business *108*

Spreading Your Brand 110

Outreach 111

Search Engine Optimization (SEO) 111

Social Media 112

Billing Concerns *115*

What are Medicaid's NEMT regulations? 115

Why do they cover NEMT? 117

Ways to Collect Payments...118

Conclusion..120

PERSONAL THANKS

I would like to thank my dear friend Buddy Carver. He has been in the NEMT business for many years. I appreciate his guidance and support, and he has been an invaluable mentor to me.

Also, I would like to thank my friend Cindy Lee. Thank you for always listening to me and my crazy schemes.

Last, but not least, I want to take a second to thank you, the reader of this book, for your support. I am happy to pass on my knowledge about this essential industry.

WHAT IS NON-EMERGENCY MEDICAL TRANSPORTATION (NEMT)?

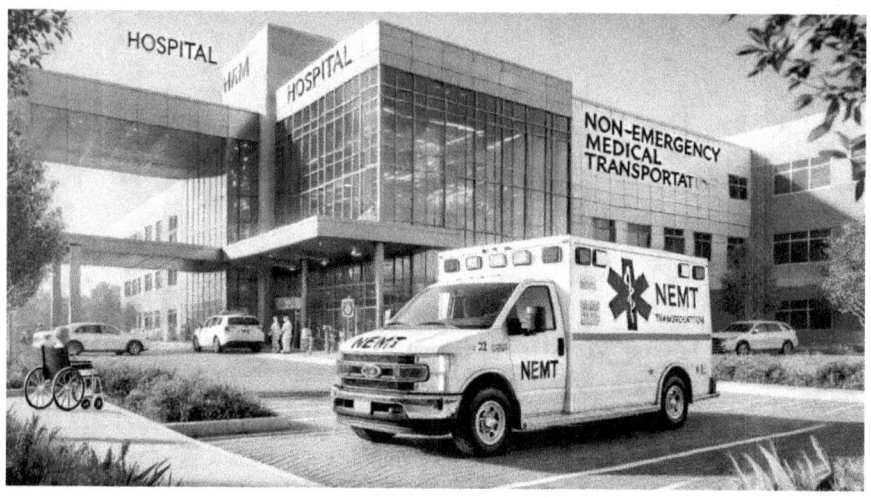

Patients need to have access to reliable and consistent care. Among the populations facing transportation barriers, the core solution for healthcare access is non-emergency medical transportation.

A major benefit of Medicaid is the ability to receive non-emergency medical transportation. However, it can be tricky to have a clear understanding of what this entails since Medicaid programs often come under question.

From state to state, what are the differences in their non-emergency medical transportation programs? What are the responsibilities of other healthcare providers in caring for patient needs?

NEMT Defined

NEMT, or non-emergency medical transportation, involves transportation services provided to healthcare consumers and patients who experience extraordinary barriers in getting to healthcare appointments.

These barriers include:

- Mental issues
- Cognitive functioning
- Physical or mental limitations
- Difficulty in waiting for services alone or traveling alone
- Not having access to a vehicle that can accommodate their disability

- The patient does not hold a valid driver's license

The purpose of NEMT is mainly for medical appointments. Without immediate treatment, any occasion that places the life and health of the Medicaid beneficiary at severe risk is an emergency. When there is an immediacy in a beneficiary's medical needs, the real emergencies happen. Acute symptoms can trigger a life-threatening situation like an automobile accident, heart attack, uncontrolled bleeding, or other severe distress.

Utilizing the full suitable transportation mode, both from and to the appointments, NEMT providers are required to offer transportation, including all associated transportation expenses.

OTHER NEMT SOLUTIONS

As a program that has been offered through the VA and some private insurers for more than just state Medicaid programs, non-emergency medical transportation is a crucial program.

Hospitals may need to step in to fill the care gap for patients. There is a growing recognition that enhancing support for patients and transportation access can help lower health costs and improve health outcomes even when health systems and hospitals within their purview of care delivery have not focused on transportation issues.

When they look at their community health needs assessments, it is possible for hospitals to design NEMT programs. Hospitals can determine the way out that is best appropriate for their population when they do this.

To assist patients in need of hospitals and other healthcare providers, ridesharing partnerships have been an excellent source. Using the familiar smartphone interface for patients to hail a ride, several hospitals are joining forces with companies like Lyft and Uber. Not only have these programs reduced the costs of transportation for several healthcare entities, but they have also proven financially effective.

Healthcare organizations need to understand how NEMT and transportation barriers impact patients' health as more of them answer the call to address the social determinants of health.

While there will still be gaps in care, healthcare providers need to determine the solutions to fill those gaps after they have identified them.

How NEMT Works

There are a few components to the system of non-emergency transportation.

- The patient can secure their own transportation.
- The patient can use ride-sharing services such as Lyft, Uber, or a government-managed rideshare, such as a handicapped-accessible bus service.
- The patient can coordinate transportation with a doctor or healthcare facility that runs their own transportation program.
- The patient or the doctor's office can obtain a ride via a NEMT broker.
- The patient or doctor can coordinate rides directly with a NEMT provider company.

For the purposes of this business book, I will focus on the last two options: finding and becoming a NEMT ride broker and starting and running your own NEMT fleet as a business.

NEMT Broker

Trained NEMT brokers administer non-emergency medical transportation services. Part of their job includes matching the request for transport with a suitable vehicle to accommodate the rider's needs.

Some of these special needs might include loading a mobility scooter or wheelchair off and onto the vehicle with the patient. They also book, schedule, and qualify riders.

They ensure clients receive professional service by ensuring that their transport providers and drivers have proper training, the latest insurance, and proper licensing. Setting up a service for clients looking for NEMT services only takes a few steps.

Here is how the process works:

The client will call a NEMT call center and provide the necessary information to the broker, including the location, time, and date of transport, as well as any appropriate information, such as other payment options or Medicaid coverage.

The call center rep will match demanded rides with vehicles and drivers who can accommodate every request for transport. The broker then uses their specialized scheduling software.

The broker then verifies payment arrangements, creating a listing on the schedule for the transportation. The scheduling software will send confirmation to the client and the driver.

At the requested time and at the chosen location, the client meets with the transporter. The transaction is completed when the patient's ride request is fulfilled by the NEMT driver.

NEMT Fleet

Often, NEMT businesses will employ their own "broker" or call center operator to take calls and schedule rides for patients. In this case, the business handles its own logistics of vetting drivers, keeping appropriate vehicles running well, and filing claims with insurance.

The NEMT business is in charge of ensuring compliance with all ADA regulations regarding transportation rules for non-emergency special needs patients.

In the healthcare sector, non-emergency medical transportation (NEMT) is becoming more essential. Each week, hundreds of thousands of people schedule NEMT rides to move from and to medical services. As a result, many of these people would not be able to access the medical services vital to their health without NEMT transportation.

THE HISTORY OF NEMT

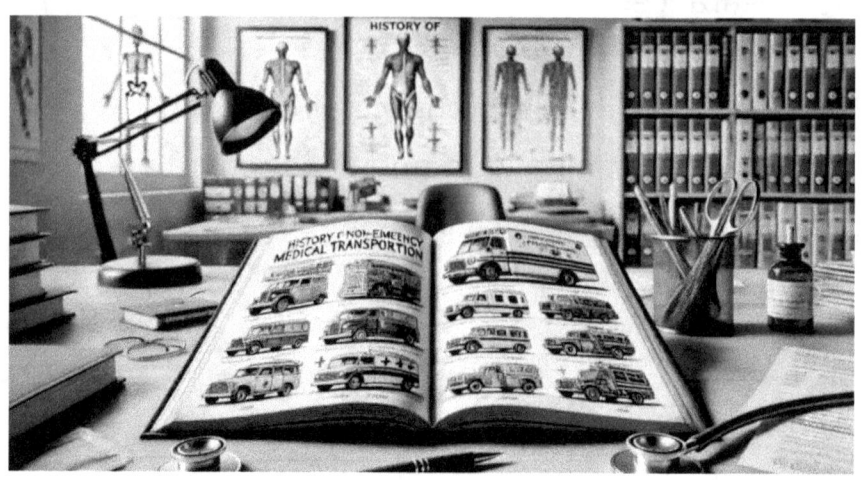

In 1965, each state was mandated to include a "provision for assuring transportation of recipients to and from providers of services." Since the establishment of Medicaid, ensuring access to medical transportation for disadvantaged populations has been a crucial responsibility for the government.

Over time, the financing and administration of the benefit have changed, even while, during the past half-century, states have regularly acknowledged the value of non-emergency medical transportation.

The Department of Health and Human Services, HHS, had the role of providing transportation for "needy" populations through the states in the early days. HHS published guidelines during the year after 1965, and they want the states to comply with the instructions for transportation assistance programs.

For its failure to provide adequate transportation to medical services, a patient who has cerebral palsy filed a class-action lawsuit against the state of Texas in the early 1970s. The case verdict, *Smith v. Vowell* 1974, reprimanded the medical assistance program of Texas for its shortsighted policies and affirmed the responsibility of the state to ensure access to transportation.

According to Senior District Judge Clary, the minor medical problem becomes a major problem when it is untreated, and as a result, and with consummate irony, someone who has no initial qualification for transportation becomes sick enough to qualify as an emergency case to be transported by ambulance, owing to those very policies, to be admitted as a hospital inpatient.

It is the worst type of false economy. Even to the state, the deprivation of medically necessary transportation is disadvantageous since it only results in higher medical costs.

Further guidance on transportation requirements emerged from federal regulators in 1978, which declared that the entire goal of a state Medicaid program is inhibited at the start unless needy individuals can get to and from service providers. Enabling the effective delivery of care saves costs. This was an early victory for NEMT, in addition to the opinion of the judge in Texas.

In 2009, Dr. Sara Rosenbaum, a renowned expert on Medicaid policy and reform, wrote that the courts and HHS had recognized the fundamental importance of assistance in transportation to program efficiency and quality for almost 45 years.

For the states to know about designing Medicaid benefits, Congress passed the Deficit Reduction Act in 2005. Operating under a fixed budget, a broker could get the job of the daily management of transportation from states, instead of a fee-for-service amount, especially for NEMT.

As for brokers that subcontract ride requests to a network of transportation providers such as para-transit companies, van fleets, taxis, and many more, several states have chosen to go into agreements with them in the decade since.

There was not enough flexibility to accommodate the patient's needs and increased enrollment. This new trend had eroded patients' choice of transportation provider, according to some critics. Also, for patients who could obtain rides, there was improved service quality and cost control with the rise of broker-managed transportation.

In the Medicaid world, during the past 25 years, an even more fundamental shift has taken place with the rise of Managed Care Organizations (MCOs). For the traditional fee-for-service Medicaid coverage, they took on the risk for a population of beneficiaries by receiving a capitated payment from the state.

Today, MCOs cover about 75 percent of Medicaid beneficiaries, compared to 10 percent in 1991. The program rolls have grown to more than 70 million today, compared to about 27 million over the same period.

With Medicaid eligibility under the Affordable Care Act up to 138 percent of the federal poverty level, much of that program growth has been recent. Some brokers are struggling to keep up with the new members who have increased the demand for NEMT in states that have opted to expand Medicaid.

Indiana and Iowa are the two states that received permission to temporarily withhold transportation benefits from the Medicaid expansion population, except for "medically frail" beneficiaries who will receive NEMT services. This will create a natural experiment that will enable officials to measure how a lack of transportation impacts costs and access.

THE EVOLUTION OF NEMT

A report by Hughes-Cromwich & Wallace indicates that, due to transportation barriers, about 3.6 million adults delay or miss non-emergency medical care yearly.

Each year, for health systems, the results of these patient no-shows have severe consequences.

There has been an evolution in non-emergency medical transportation to combat this startling statistic. Guarantee that getting to and from the care provider is accessible for patients, and overcome this care barrier.

Even though most of the offerings available today remain quite limited in terms of capabilities, vendors are rolling out NEMT solutions to meet market demand and contribute to the spike the industry is witnessing.

In 2019, here are three crucial predictions, as there is a continuous recognition of the full potential of NEMT:

- The need for NEMT services will increase awareness.

- There will be an increasing move of care away from traditional care settings.

- Throughout the healthcare ecosystem, further insight into data around how, why, and where of patients' movement, there will be an amplified need.

Increased Awareness of the Need for NEMT Services

Throughout the system, managing and addressing the flow of patients is a significant challenge that healthcare organizations are currently facing.

According to a current study, for some patients to see their healthcare provider, more than 85 percent of patients reported waiting 10 to 30 minutes past their scheduled appointment time.

The critical components to improving patient flow and minimizing wait times are interfacility ambulance transportation and streamlined NEMT.

In 2019, managed care organizations, accountable care organizations, hospitals, and several other healthcare settings will realize how NEMT flows throughout care settings and how significant it is to their patient treatment.

Moving Care Beyond Traditional Settings

There is a rise in patients receiving home treatment as healthcare progressively grows into a consumer-centric model.

Community paramedicine and home healthcare are the first cases of this, where patients get their care wherever suitable for them or directly at home. At present, there are several additional logistics regarding providing and managing care instead of discharging transportation requirements and coordinating patient admission.

These days, physicians and nurses disregard the customary healthcare locales and go into care settings and homes. As a result, proper logistics must be coordinated around vendors, care providers, and patients.

Providers must begin to consider utilizing the conveniences of software solutions for logistics management related to the provision of care. An all-encompassing platform, in an automated manner and through one dashboard, coordinates all communications and transportation logistics.

Throughout the network of healthcare, and for further insight into data, there will be an amplified need for information on how, why, and where they are moving patients

Improving operations, analytics, reporting, and data within the healthcare ecosystem is increasingly becoming more significant. Ahead of proper care delivery to a patient, healthcare organizations now need to know:

- What is the clinical diagnosis of the patient?
- What methods of transportation are patients utilizing?
- What does the transportation cost?
- Did the patient go out of network to get treated by a physician?
- What were the causes of the throughput delays for the patient?

When choosing a NEMT partner, healthcare providers must look for a program that possesses the capacity to capture data, given these transportation's logistics and questions.

Healthcare organizations can identify negative trends before they become problems when they have an in-depth understanding of the information related to transportation and discharge delays.

They can construct more informed clinical and operational assessments around service level agreements and contracts.

As a result, healthcare providers can make space for capable vehicles and clinical resources, improving overall patient satisfaction and care, increasing efficiency, and ultimately streamlining operations to enable cost-saving.

As healthcare organizations continue to recognize the full benefits of offering NEMT services, 2019 is expected to be the beginning of pivotal years ahead.

THE STATE OF THE NEMT INDUSTRY

Patients may find it challenging to get to their medical appointments. Finding transportation can be quite challenging, particularly for frail patients and the elderly.

Suppose you have the dream of launching your own non-emergency medical transportation business. In that case, you will learn how advanced technologies can help your business and how you can help providers better manage their time and also improve how your patients can get the care they need.

Because they lack affordable or available transportation, more than 3.6 million individuals delay or miss care every year. This is a serious healthcare issue in our country, as the nation's healthcare system loses an estimated $150 billion annually because of missed medical appointments.

As a result, it is imperative to help healthcare providers clear hurdles. NEMT patients, many of whom are vulnerable and frail, can utilize advanced technologies to get help and have access to the care they need.

Care coordinators and providers are now monitoring patients' travel to medical appointments and managing their time in scheduling with the help of emerging technologies. They should focus adequately on the patient's care instead of worrying about when patients will arrive.

Digitally integrated transportation networks are setting the stage for this advancement. These technological advancements create smooth trip assignments and a ride schedule. The software can contact patients, caregivers, case managers, healthcare facilities, and call centers and enable automated administration of transportation benefits.

With the inclusion of GPS tracking, every ride can be digitally tracked. When a patient is picked up or dropped off, a dashboard can be created for care coordinators and facilities to see the patient and events that happen during the journey.

As a result, care coordinators can now provide the appropriate treatment regimens as they navigate the several facets of their patient's non-emergency medical transportation with the aid of this actionable, real-time data.

COST REDUCTIONS

Healthcare providers and patient care coordinators now have the information at their fingertips through a dashboard that provides the estimated time rather than calling a transportation provider or a cab company to determine when a patient will arrive.

In the space of NEMT, when taking a holistic view of emerging technologies, another factor to highlight is the reduction of service providers' costs and increased accessibility.

Since more than 95 percent of care coordinators have to work through a combination of vouchers and receipts from a network of transport providers and cab companies, they have no idea of how much time they spend on the tedious bookkeeping connected with transportation costs. The evaluation process becomes increasingly cumbersome for them, as well as impossible for them to have any perspective on it in a concise and clear format, because it's not at the aggregate level. At present, they have availability for easy access since it is housed in one place with the new technology.

In the NEMT business, it is essential to engage technology-based solutions that offer a high overall system and improved functionality to enhance access for people in need and for service providers to reduce barriers to healthcare transportation. Advanced technology provides a giant step forward.

CHANGES IN HEALTHCARE TRANSPORTATION

It is unfortunate that 3.6 million Americans still delay or miss their medical appointments every year because of transportation problems.

It is with the brokers of NEMT that the large part of the transport budget of the country is allocated, since, whenever required, having the right to the benefit of transportation as Medicaid beneficiaries is their responsibility.

However, throughout the country, abuse of the benefit, waste, and fraud are rampant. Patients are left stranded after appointments, drivers arrive hours late, and rides never show up, even when they are scheduled.

Over the past five years, consumer expectations have dramatically transformed through the recent rideshare models and technologically enabled transportation services.

NEMT brokers must modernize and share information with providers, and they can be even more efficient by utilizing technology, tablets, and GPS tracking.

BRAND AND CUSTOMER AWARENESS

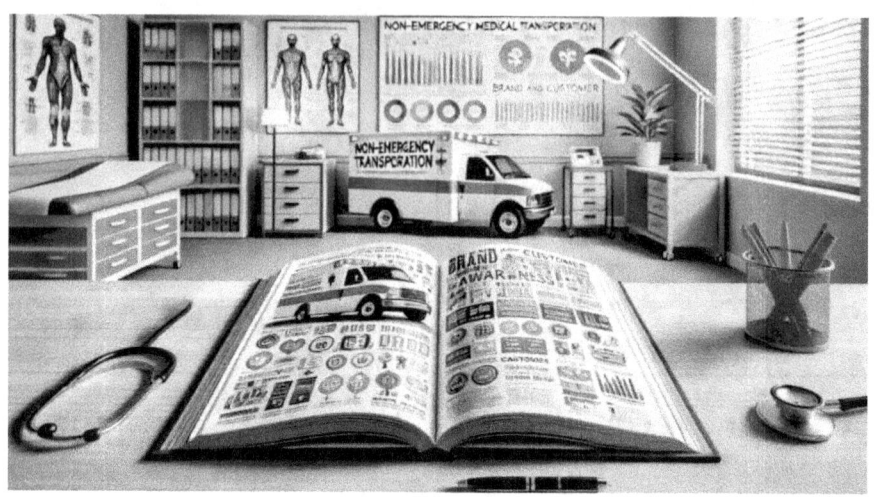

During the course of starting your business, you will have to make some decisions. Consider the answer to these questions, based on your area and market for the services you want to offer:

- Where will you be located?
- What areas will you service?
- What types of transportation will you provide?
- Who will be your targeted customers?
- What need will you meet with your new business venture?
- What experience do you have in this area?

The way you choose to answer these questions will direct the way your business operates. Your vision and mission for your business are the basis for what defines how you do what you do.

LOCATION

When considering a location, consider whether you want to run this business from your home. While your customers won't necessarily be visiting your business in a storefront fashion, your business will still need a physical address for your business license.

Consider local zoning laws and regulations for running home-based businesses in your area.

If you're renting, does your lease allow you to run a business from your home?

If you choose to open an office, consider the costs involved in leasing a space, filling it with the applicable office equipment, utilities, and possibly staffing the space.

Ultimately, you will also have to have a place to store your work vehicle. This will probably start with just one vehicle, but think about when you expand your fleet. Where will you have room to park your work car(s) that are secure?

For the sake of saving you gas and travel miles, think of a location in your area that is more convenient to access major roadways, hospitals, or an elderly population. If a major travel route commonly includes a highway, you might want to consider being located near where you can easily access the highway.

Wherever your base of operations becomes, think about how far you're willing to drive to take clients. Perhaps you could take a map and draw out a circumference of how far you're willing to drive. Pizza delivery drivers do this. They have an area near their restaurant and addresses within a certain distance that they will serve.

You may want to consider drawing a boundary line of sorts for areas that you are willing to serve. This may also include a list of not just general street addresses, but doctors' offices, hospitals, clinics, and testing facilities. Think about places you will often be taking clients to and think about routes you might take. If you can save on mileage, that's a cost-saving for your business.

TYPES OF TRANSPORTATION

There are different services you can offer in the transportation sector. While the term "NEMT" is rather broad, you can consider narrowing the types of customers you will serve.

Types of transportation in this industry include:

- Ambulatory (able to walk) patient transport
- Intensive care patient transport
- Mental health transport
- Incubator transport
- Airport shuttle
- Nursing care centers
- Medical centers
- Hospitals
- Private paying clients
- Wheelchair or stretcher transport (paratransport)

If you're considering offering wheelchair or stretcher transport, in a non-emergency capacity, then the vehicle you choose for your business must meet certain requirements.

This would be to reach patients who are bound to a wheelchair full-time or who need to be transported via stretcher. These sorts of patients may be very ill or may be severely disabled.

The ADA (Americans with Disabilities Act) dictates that vehicles used for paratransit must meet specific parameters to be considered appropriately wheelchair accessible.

- They must have a 56" door opening height.
- A handicap lift with a 30" x 40" wide clear platform.
- Wheelchair attachments that are able to withstand 2,500 pounds of pressure per leg.
- Seat belt mechanism with 4-point tie-downs with lap and shoulder belts.
- Interior lighting is one foot-candle of illumination.

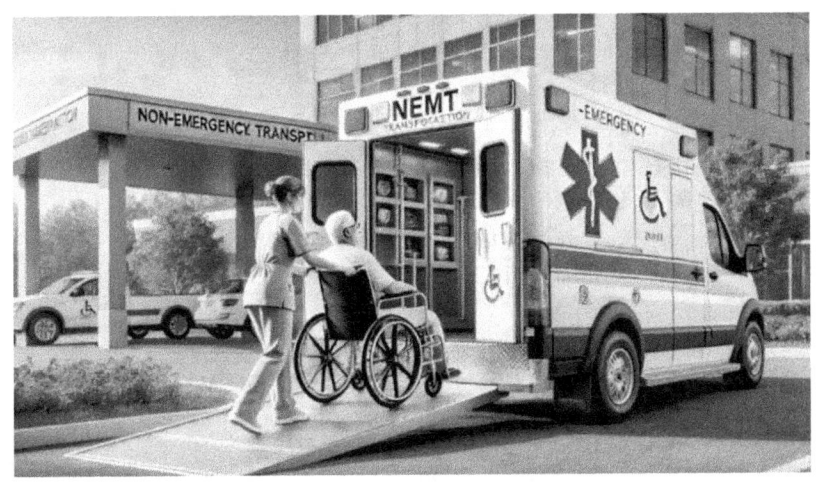

Even if you are considering only offering services to clients who can walk, or may use an assistive device to walk, you should consider how easy it is to get in and out of your vehicle.

Good vehicles for patient transport include minivans, larger sedans, and SUVs. Your clients will most likely be elderly, frail, sick, or just not 100%. Consider the comforts you can offer them while they are in your care, riding in your car.

You may want to have umbrellas, water bottles, mints, throw-up bags, blankets, or small snacks available for your clients. Simple comfort items can make a difference to your customers and set you apart from other service providers.

GAUGE YOUR EXPERIENCE

Do you have a clean driving record?

Do you enjoy helping people?

To get started, these are really the only qualifications that you need!

You may want to consider getting basic CPR and First Aid training and certification from the American Red Cross. Affordable classes are often held at hospitals and community centers, and you can even get a certification online at https://www.redcross.org/.

There is no specialized training or certifications for the NEMT industry, but there is an agency that you can gain certification with to appear more professional. It is not a requirement, but it is a check on your business that will attract customers, knowing that you are compliant with the agency's regulations.

For your NEMT business to decrease liability and serve as a market differentiator, it needs to pass through the Non-Emergency Medical Transportation

Accreditation Commission, NEMTAC (https://www.nemtac.org/). This is a program designed to promote and enhance the quality of care in America's medical transportation system as the only national accreditation program.

You will be able to distinguish your business by having an industry standard of excellence. The accreditation process for NEMTAC can be comprehensive, and, apart from its design to increase utilization, it exceeds those established by state or local regulators.

By going online, you can get the application form on the NEMTAC website, fill in the required spaces, and submit. As it can be comprehensible, the entire process of accreditation can take between 45 and 90 days.

In some cases, they can expedite the process by moving faster and working with your company. $75 is the application fee for all organizations, and as for the accreditation fee, it begins at $750 per organization. The accreditation is valid for three years. Generally, some respective documentation and categories NEMTAC will review include:

- Call center operations/communications
- Safety management
- Vehicle maintenance
- Risk management
- Quality improvement
- Compliance program
- Personnel management
- Financial management
- Organizational management

NEMTAC-accredited services must be part of what your business provides, including stretcher and wheelchair van services, medical ride-sharing programs, paratransit providers, and non-emergency medical transportation services. You may have to contact them if your business offers healthcare that doesn't match those listed above or services under an emerging model of medical transportation.

For Medicaid/Medicare transports, it is necessary to provide the National Provider Identifier (NPI). You will also have to provide your company's EIN and any other licenses required by your city or state.

A GREAT START

This all may seem very overwhelming. May I suggest one way to get started?

Start as a senior transport business.

Your target customers can be seniors who either can't or don't drive for whatever reason. They still need to get to and from doctor appointments, and they appreciate having the company of a competent and courteous driver.

You may also be available to drive them to other errands, social events, and family gatherings that they may not have other transportation to attend. For this type of client, it's more than just being a taxi or Uber.

The best thing about providing a senior transportation service is that you can do a lot of things that taxi cabs and community buses won't be able to, and that is where your new business fits in.

For example, you will be able to provide what is commonly referred to as 'door-through-door' service, which means you enter the client's home, assist them in leaving the house, and then enter your waiting vehicle.

You then take them to their appointment, assisting them from the vehicle to their destination. You can wait there for them, then once the appointment is complete, repeat the procedure but in reverse.

Here are the steps to get started in this lucrative and much-needed niche. We'll talk about these steps in detail in a subsequent chapter.

- Start with your own car.

- Create a brand name and a logo. Display it in your car, on a shirt that you wear as a "uniform," and anywhere that you talk about your business.

- Can start at your home office.

- Get accounting software.

- Have a dedicated business phone line, probably a cell phone since you'll rarely be at the office during working hours.

- Have trip logging software.

- Get scheduling software or apps.

- Create a business plan.
- Obtain an EIN.
- Open a business bank account.
- Obtain a business license for your locality.
- Register your business (an LLC is most common).
- Set your prices (look at the local market and be competitive).
- Learn how to bill insurance/Medicaid.
- Get the word out with word of mouth, flyers, doctor's offices, senior care centers, retirement homes, and by leaving business cards everywhere.
- Create a website with your business name as the URL. You can hire someone to do this for you, or you can use a site like Squarespace (https://www.squarespace.com/).
- Get on social media! Grab your chosen business name on every social media platform. The big ones are Facebook (with a growing population of seniors, who are your target audience), Twitter, and Instagram. You will also want to claim your Google business listing page for clients to leave reviews.

This is just the beginning. As your business grows, you can gain more cars and drivers, offering even more services as you see the need arise for them. Filling a need to find the gap in this industry in your area is important.

Writing a Business Plan for Your NEMT Business

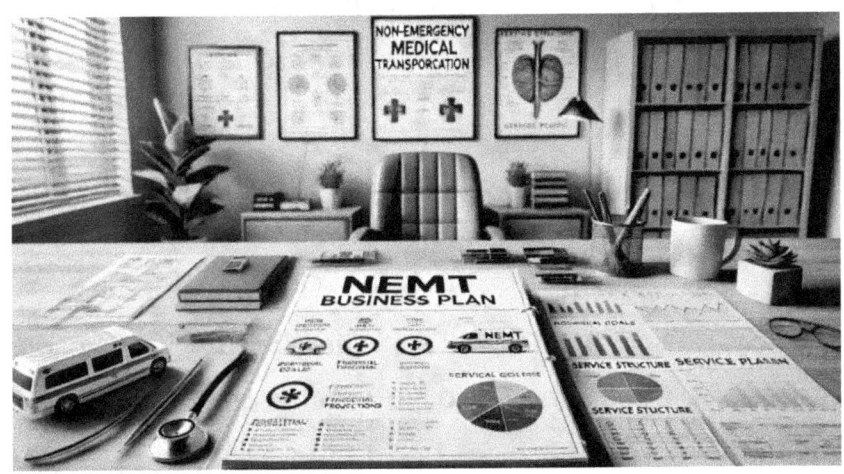

As an entrepreneur myself, it amazes me all the time to meet quite several entrepreneurs with an outdated business plan or even without one at all. According to them, it is when someone is seeking a loan or an investor that a business plan becomes necessary. Indeed, a business plan is much more than just a financial device.

When you plan to hold yourself accountable for your business's success, progress monitoring, and organization, a business plan is all you need to achieve these crucial elements.

Fundamentally, when crafting a business plan, there's never a wrong time to create one. Whether you have developed your business for years or you are making adequate preparations to launch one, a business plan is for you.

Also, if you have an existing business plan, there's nothing wrong with periodically updating or reviewing it. As your business grows, changes, and progresses over time, and your business plan needs to reflect such growth and changes as a living document.

For those who find it hard to transport themselves to healthcare facilities or medical appointments, they enjoy the much-needed services of non-emergency medical transportation companies. Therefore, a business plan is quite essential before you think of jumping into the transportation business.

Outlining a detailed business plan can help you determine the market's profitability and how to run the company with the required staff and vehicles.

Why You Should Have a Business Plan

Here are some of the reasons to have a business plan for your business:

Action Plan

For any business owner, a business plan is a useful document. However, you will be creating a living, breathing document that will give you the direction you need to go, as well as outlining where you are and where you want to be in the future.

Think of a business plan as a roadmap to success. Writing a business plan sounds like a daunting task, but it shouldn't be. Just be clear and concise.

Keep it short. No one is going to read hundreds of pages that you have slaved over. Start with a cover page, followed by a Table of Contents, and then go on from there.

GENERATING NEW IDEAS

From the depths of the business planning process, some of the best things emerge. You can gain insight from fresh perspectives and different approaches and discover new ideas.

A business plan is not a structured, stiff, and lengthy document, despite its sometimes negative reputation.

Indeed, the opposite is an effective business plan. Against some of the toughest business challenges, you can come up with new solutions and think creatively through the elements of a dynamic, growing, and flexible business plan. This is particularly true when you consider the section regarding marketing strategy.

REALITY CHECK

Writing a business plan is often the first real struggle for small business owners who attempt to launch a new venture.

Some of them may not want to consider that their business idea is not yet fully developed or may a bit flawed.

As a business owner, you can identify gaps early on in the process, take steps to make your business more viable and stronger, test your ideas, and better refine your research. Before you make any investment, whether of time or money with a business idea that is likely to fail, there may be an initial setback, but any further work can bolster your chance of success.

Decision Making

If you are not fully committed, undecided, or on the fence at a certain point, you cannot complete some sections in a traditional business plan.

Since it is imperative to write specific information down in black and white, business plans help you eliminate the gray area. One of the most useful parts of writing a business plan, and also one of the hardest aspects, is making tough decisions.

For example, the services section of your business plan will be difficult to complete if you haven't specifically decided what services your business will offer at what price points.

It's a Necessity

A business plan is required if you enlist a business partner's support, pitch to investors about your business idea, apply for a small business grant or loan, or have a plan to approach a financial institution for a loan.

Supporters and potential investors want to see facts and figures in black and white to gauge the true potential of your business. The only acceptable and best way for you to provide this information is through a business plan.

Ultimately, you should understand that you don't need to have all the answers while you wait to get started.

If you are using your plan as a valid business planning tool, you can continue with your planning and startup momentum while you fill in all of the necessary data you have at present, and you start an outline of your plan now.

Then, as you learn more about the market, you can work on filling in the blanks. Along your journey to business success, you will realize that a business plan can be invaluable as a flexible and fluid document.

PARTS OF A BUSINESS PLAN

For the next three to five years, a roadmap for your non-medical transportation business is a business plan, and some of the essential elements it needs to include are:

EXECUTIVE SUMMARY

The entire plan's synopsis is where you can start the document. The last thing people write is the executive summary, even when it is often the first element of a business plan.

In your one-page executive summary (or less), you must add a summary of how you want the business to grow, highlights of the business growth so far, a description of your services, basics about when your company was founded, and your mission statement.

Here is an example:

Our Mission

Senior Shuttles offers superior senior transportation services to the greater metropolitan area. We ensure that our clients get to where they need to go, specializing in non-emergency medical transport in a safe, caring, and comfortable environment.

The Company and Management

Senior Shuttles is headquartered in the City of West Vancouver and incorporated in the Province of British Columbia. It is owned by partners Susie Quinn and Cindy Lee. Susie has extensive experience in senior care, while Cindy has worked in sales and marketing for 15 years.

The management of Senior Shuttles consists of co-owners Susie Quinn and Cindy Lee. Both partners will be taking hands-on management roles in the company.

Our Services

Our clients are senior citizens who can't or no longer wish to drive. Senior Shuttles offers a comprehensive door-to-door service to seniors, including:

- Scheduling rides for appointments
- Assisting with pick up, escorting the client from their home to the car
- Assisting the client with getting in the vehicle

- Providing amenities during the ride, such as a blanket, water, music of the client's choice, and stowage of their walking assistance apparatus
- Assisting the client with disembarking from the vehicle
- Assisting the client with entering the building at their destination, waiting with the client as needed
- Repeating the process in reverse as relevant

The Market

Across Canada, the senior transportation business has seen explosive growth over the last three years. West Vancouver is an affluent area with a high density of people over the age of 55. Our market research has shown that 7 out of 10 seniors in West Vancouver would prefer to have a car and driver to help them get to necessary doctor appointments.

Our Competitive Advantages

While there are currently eight businesses offering at-call transportation services in West Vancouver, only three of these specifically offer senior transport, and none offer the amenities and through-the-door service that we have outlined.

All employees are insured and bonded.

Financial Projections

Based on the size of our market and our defined market area, our sales projections for the first year are $120,000. We project a growth rate of 10 percent per year for the first three years.

The salary for each of the co-owners will be $40,000. At startup, we will only have the two managers running the business. Co-owner Susie Quinn will schedule appointments and coordinate services, but we plan to hire a full-time receptionist this year as well.

Already, we have service commitments from over 40 clients and plan to aggressively build our client base through newspaper ads, a branded website, social media, and direct mail advertising. The loving on-site professional care that Senior Shuttles will provide is sure to benefit seniors throughout the West Vancouver area.

Startup Financing Requirements

We are seeking an operating line of $150,000 to finance our first-year growth. Together, the co-owners have invested $62,000 to meet working capital requirements.

COMPANY DESCRIPTION

You have to elaborate on what your business is about here. You should define what your non-emergency transport business will offer, what sets you apart from your competitors, your differences, and who you serve.

This section will take care of your business's "why" and "what" so that readers can understand your extended elevator pitch better. Also, add more description about any competitive advantages that have made or will make you successful, the specific types of customers your business serves, how, in the marketplace, your business will satisfy particular needs, and ultimately, what your company does.

Here is an example:

The mission of Senior Shuttles is to provide quality non-emergency medical transportation services to ambulatory members of the senior community in our area.

The Senior Shuttles office will be located at 200 Cypress Bowl Lane W, Vancouver BC V7S 3H9.

The business will be an LLC owned and operated by Susie Quinn and Cindy Lee.

We will be a full-service "through the door" transportation service aimed at senior citizens aged 55+ who either choose not to drive or cannot drive any longer due to physical constraints. In 2016, more than two in five people in Vancouver were over the age of 65, and that number is expected to rise as our population grows older overall.

Within three years, we plan to expand to offer a wheelchair accessible van paratransit service. At five years, we plan to add an ambulance service that can accommodate stretcher transport.

Service will be provided to and from the client's home to doctors' offices and major hospitals in many areas. We will also consider transport to medical testing facilities and cancer treatment centers.

We will be open

Monday through Thursday from 8:00 am to 7:00 pm,

Friday from 7:00 am to Noon.

Saturday hours would be by special appointment only.

OPERATING EXPENSES

If you are planning to offer certain kinds of services, list them in detail, including picking up patients at healthcare facilities, at assisted living facilities, or at their homes.

The manner with which you plan to provide these services needs to be part of your explanations, such as contracting with Medicaid and registering with your state.

Also, what types of licensing do you require, like local city requirements for offering medical transportation services and special state permits?

The required insurance policies, such as vehicle and liability coverage, must also be part of your description. What you need to run the business, including hydraulic lifts to meet the specific needs of your clients and vehicles that meet the safety regulations of your state, must also be in your discussion.

MARKET ANALYSIS

Right away, it is time to take a deeper dive into your industry. Here, you determine what share of the non-medical business market you can capture, as well as provide and identify details about the non-emergency medical transportation, including the purchasing trends, demographics, forecasted and historical growth rates, and the size.

Your market is not everyone. Therefore, your market research and analysis have the goal of identifying your market segments. A segment is a group of people within your market that will buy your product or service. Each of the segments is your target market.

A good business plan not only identifies the target market but also breaks it down into segments and includes data showing how fast each will grow from many angles.

Here is the methodology:

TAM: Total Available Market. How big is the entire market to which you could provide a product or service? For instance, the entire city where our fictitious business is located has a population of over 600,000 people.

SAM: Segmented Available Market. This is the group you will target from the TAM data. For instance, Senior Shuttles will be on the west side of the city's main county.

SOM: Share of Market. This subset is who you could actually reach in the first year or so of being in business. This number is extrapolated from SAM. How many of those 600,000 people can you reach and convince to spend their money on your services?

While you are putting together the numbers and size of your market segments, also research the potential growth of each. How many senior citizens remain in the area? How fast is the target area growing per year, in percentages? Is it in decline?

COMPETITIVE ANALYSIS

In this section, you will make competition assessments of non-emergency medical transportation.

What are the weaknesses and strengths of your competitors?

Are they attempting to accomplish anything?

What are the manners in which they take the market for their businesses?

Can you take advantage of specific opportunities to be competitive?

What are the barriers you need to overcome?

When you discuss the competition, talk about who is offering the same services or providing the same products. Other businesses want to solve your customers' problems, too.

How is what you are going to offer better? What is your advantage?

Discuss how, in your environment, you will create a better, more successful business. This is also called the value proposition.

Discuss a little of the history of the industry, profitability, and the health of the overall industry. You don't have to write a book, but put together several paragraphs or a timeline pointing out the milestones.

In fact, this book has already provided you with a little history of the NEMT market and the current state of it. Do your own research, especially as it applies to your specific area.

What are the trends? Why? Who are these people, and what is their price point?

Projected Loss and Income Statements

You must show your expenses and the manner in which you plan to use to pay for these expenses as you develop expected loss and income statements.

This would include expenses such as ambulances and vans, as well as any specialized equipment that accompanies them. Include the benefits and wages you plan to pay your drivers, as well as costs for equipment like computers, various office equipment, and necessary software to track and schedule payments for transportation.

Since this will determine your profit and help you grow your business as you pay for your expenses, calculate the weekly number of clients you need to transport.

Generally, your company's financial health and future must be part of this section. While they need to be grounded in reality, you may also include expected gross income or other economic predictions.

Outline your liabilities and assets with the use of the balance sheets, reports of cash flow, and income statements. This section of your business plan needs to be detailed, accurate, and current, as it is critical if you are seeking funding.

PROMOTIONAL AND MARKETING PLAN

Here, you will need to discover ways to promote your business, including getting registered as a business with the state. When government agencies work with individuals who need transportation services, they can provide your contact information.

Advertise your transportation services to medical offices as well as assisted and retirement living facilities.

Provide presentations to local senior citizen community groups.

Sign up for a business listing with websites that help people find transportation, like Paratransit Watch.

When people search for medical transportation services online, have your business appear by listing on Google Maps.

Define your sales and marketing strategies by explaining how you will find and create customers. Explain your procedure on communication as well as where and how your messaging will be shared for marketing.

What are the methods your business will use to identify, attract, and convert leads? Who will handle sales, and how will you train any outside help for sales?

Detailing your marketing and advertising plans should be done by the product lifecycle. Know each cycle, the benefits, changes, types, and channels of advertising you will use.

For instance, in the introductory stage, most of your focus will be on building brand awareness. You may use discounts and coupons to attract customers, but your big investments will be in advertising and digital marketing. You must engage as many people as possible to create demand through promotion.

In the growth stage, most businesses spend more on brand equity and preference. More dollars are spent on advertising and digital content than were spent in the introduction phase. More money should be coming in, justifying the expense, and public relations should support the advertising.

In the maturity life cycle, the marketing and advertising focus shifts to capturing the competitors' market share by getting customers to be brand loyal to you. Also, the maturity stage can be an introductory stage for various new lines, products, and services you add to your business.

It becomes harder to acquire new customers. Therefore, you have to keep sales from slipping by keeping existing customers satisfied. Retain loyal customers with ongoing campaigns to get feedback through email and newsletters. Use these and other promotional channels to provide information that enhances the benefits of your product or service.

We will discuss more marketing and advertising in a later chapter.

OPERATIONS AND MANAGEMENT

Have an in-depth discussion on the operations of your business. Also, include the number of employees, your management team's profiles, ownership information, and the structure of your organization.

Provide as much background information as possible for key players and a detailed description of who does what in your business, regardless of whether your business is a sole proprietorship or a small business.

To provide services daily and operate your business, you also need to elaborate on the employees and management you plan to hire. What are the education and qualifications of your operations manager, including experience in the medical transportation field, a business background, and medical training? You may also want to describe the drivers you intend to hire, including those who have medical training with clean records.

This section describes your management team and staff and how business ownership is structured.

Readers want to know who is on your team, what their skills are, and what they can contribute to the bottom line.

Break this section into four parts:

1. Ownership Structure

2. Internal Management

3. External Management

4. Human Resources Needs

Ownership

This is the legal structure of your business. It has been discussed in other parts of the plan, but review it here in this section. You want to define who holds what percent ownership in the company clearly.

Internal Management

The following are the main business management categories. Use the ones pertinent to your business and how you want things to run.

- Sales
- Marketing
- Administration
- Drivers/hands-on staff
- Human Resources

Identify the people who have the main responsibility for each category and their skills, and include their resumes. It is not necessary to have one person per category; for instance, one key person can fill many roles.

You, for example, are in sales, marketing, and production. Your partner or family member could be in human resources and administration.

Identify key people. The bigger your company, the more key people and categories you will need. Deduce what and who you need based on your business and the size of the business you are starting. You may begin with a few people and add others along the way.

In our fake business, Senior Shuttles, we will have just the two starting partners as employees. Susie Q. will handle administration and human resources (i.e., hiring staff), and Cindy L. will handle sales (call center) and marketing since she has the most previous experience with this.

This internal management plan results in your management team's outline. Discuss salary, benefits, profit-sharing, and non-compete agreements.

MARKET POTENTIAL AND TARGET MARKET

What is the market potential, including the non-emergency medical transportation plan created for your municipality?

This part of your business plan will discuss the reasons why your clients will use your service. These reasons can include limited mental abilities, no access to a car, or poor health. For people over the age of 65, more than one in five need access to non-emergency medical transportation.

Before you review census data for your area, this gives provision for an overall idea of the market and to further determine the market potential. Your angle is that people with disabilities or senior citizens that cannot drive to medical appointments need more help than what regular transportation services provide. Here is where you will identify the target market for your services.

FINANCIAL STATEMENTS

An income statement, also called a profit and loss statement (P&L), is a chart-form summary of your company's P&L for any given period of time. An income statement is typically prepared on a monthly basis, followed by a quarterly and annual view and comparison.

It begins with your revenue, followed by the costs section, which includes labor and materials. Finally, the last section is operating and overhead, arriving at your net profit.

The next document you should construct is called a "cash flow projection."

This defines the supply of available cash, which is your daily lifeline. Can you meet day-to-day expenses, deal with emergencies, or support a growth burst?

Often, a company can show a profit but has no ready cash. A cash flow chart projects your expenses and income.

Finally, you should provide a "balance sheet." The balance sheet lists your assets and liabilities.

Assets are items of value you own. Liabilities are your debts.

Your equity equals your assets minus your liabilities. Equity and liabilities must always equal assets.

REQUEST FOR FUNDING

If you are taking your business plan to a bank for a business loan, then you will need to include the next section in your master plan.

Tips for writing a clear and concise Request for Funding include:

- Tailor your funding request to each financial source. Lenders and investors need different information.

- Keep your funding sources in mind. Each will have different requirements. Accommodate these requests. Do research and address that information in your request.

- Ask for enough to keep the business going.

- Write in plain English. Don't use acronyms or jargon.

- Keep your project focused, and do not commit to other plans or projects you cannot deliver.

- Remain specific; do not talk in generalities. For instance, don't say something like, "We are going to have a shop to repair bikes" or "We are going to wash cars." That is not a plan, is it?

- Focus your request on the investor's priorities. Provide all the documentation they requested and all the additional information requested.

- Present evidence of the need for your business in your community.

- Meet deadlines, be on time, and dress appropriately.

- Keep your budget specific. Do not include non-specific items in the budget.

- Apply to one investor at a time. Do not put yourself in the damaging position of having to turn an investor down because of a better deal or because you chose the first investor who responded.

More Help with Writing a Business Plan

Some of you might still need more help in writing a business plan. I can understand that. Those of you that want more help to write your plan, my advice is to use a template.

As long as you understand what a business plan and all of its inner workings are, it will be easier for you to work with a template. I am sure if you spend a couple of hours on it, you will be able to have a plan ready.

Now the big question is where you might get templates. Well, if you are using Microsoft Word, then you can download many business plan templates directly from the Microsoft Office website. Just type "Microsoft Word Business Plan Templates" in any popular search engine, and you can find templates.

Long-Term Success

An integral part of a business is a business plan.

In reality, business plans are most times are responsible for creating a long list of research you still need to conduct and other work that requires completion as well as depends in part on projections with a requirement of a tremendous amount of data at your fingertips.

A good business plan concisely answers the what, when, where, who, why, and how of every aspect of your new business venture.

Keep details and each step in mind when writing your business plan. It is important to review and revise your plan. Remember that your plan is never finished. It is not a static document.

BUSINESS STRUCTURE AND FINANCES

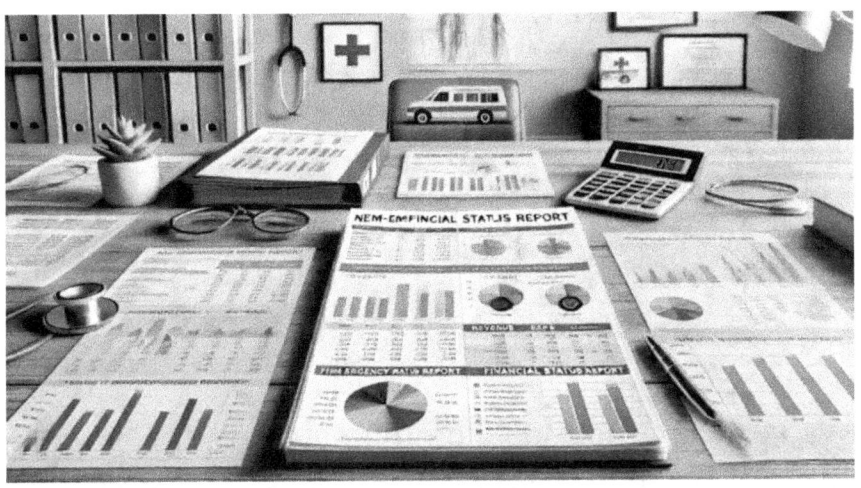

Starting a business is fun, but a little overwhelming and certainly confusing if you are unsure as to what to do next.

One of the more confusing areas is choosing a business structure. Even if you know the options, how can you know which is right for your business? In this chapter, we are going to look at the types of business structures and how you can choose the right one for your preferences.

For your business structure as non-emergency medical transportation, NEMT, you can choose one of the following:

- Partnership
- Corporation
- LLC
- Sole proprietor

SOLE PROPRIETOR

This is one of the most common structures for small businesses. The business is entirely yours, and you will assume complete responsibility. This means you get all the profits but are also liable for all losses.

A sole proprietorship is also known as a "pass-through" tax entity. This means that all profits and losses are passed through to you as the business owner, and you need to report them on your taxes.

PARTNERSHIP

When you choose to partner with someone for your business, you may choose to share ownership, so all parties involved have a share over input and participation in the company. This is still a simple business structure.

It is important to note that there are different types of partnership options. The kind you choose will depend on how long you want to be partners and what active role each party is taking in the business.

GENERAL PARTNERSHIP

Assumes all parties involved are involved equally, including all profits, liabilities, and duties. If anything is intentionally unequally split, then it needs to be noted in the official partnership agreement.

LIMITED PARTNERSHIP

This format is often used when one partner serves as an investor with limited input into the company's operations. It is more complex and typically isn't used as often unless the intention is to become a sole proprietor eventually.

JOINT VENTURE

If you are planning to partner with someone for just one specific project, then the joint venture format is best. It is similar to a general partnership, but is only for a particular period of time to complete a single project.

LIMITED LIABILITY CORPORATION (LLC)

With the two previous options, the scariest factor is that you'll be personally responsible if something goes wrong with the business, and you or your partner may not be able to pay for the resulting costs.

The LLC structure offers you the best of everything. It gives you the flexibility of the previous two structures, but limits the responsibilities of those involved, like a corporate structure.

An LLC is probably the most common business structure of any NEMT business startup. It's generally the easiest to form, register, and run tax-wise.

LLC registration requirements vary a little by state, so check with your state requirements regarding how you must form an LLC and do business in that particular state.

While choosing an LLC has many advantages, it is a more complex structure. You'll need to consider the following to determine if an LLC structure is right for you.

An LLC is considered a pass-through tax entity, like the two previous structures. However, under an LLC structure, you are only taxed on your share of the profits, which are filed under your personal taxes.

In almost all states except Massachusetts, you can form an LLC with a single individual. In some situations, starting an LLC can be a better option than starting a sole proprietorship.

Corporation

This is likely the structure most people think of when it comes to business. A corporation involves shareholders, a complex legal structure, and intricate tax requirements.

It is important to know that there are several types of corporate structures to choose from. The most common type is known as a C Corporation or C Corp.

Generally speaking, this is not the sort of business structure you should adopt for a first-time business start-up, especially if you are going at it alone or with just one other person.

Obtain an EIN

The EIN, also known as a Federal or Employer Tax Identification Number, is used to identify a business entity. You can apply for this in several ways, but most prefer online.

It is a free service offered through the Internal Revenue Service. Check with your state to determine if you need a state number or a charter.

Here is a link to the IRS website where you can download or fill out the form online:

https://www.irs.gov/businesses/small-businesses-self-employed/how-to-apply-for-an-ein

Think of an EIN as a Social Security number for your business.

BUSINESS LICENSE AND ARTICLES OF INCORPORATION

When you create an LLC, you'll have to choose a company name, file articles of organization, and create an operating agreement. You'll also need to file for specific licenses or permits and a DBA if you need one.

After making a decision about selecting your business entity (probably an LLC), your business will require licensing. If you are selling taxable merchandise, you may need a seller's permit.

You will require a federal tax ID number and also a state employer number if you decide to hire drivers or other employees. Also, if you file as an LLC or a corporation, an independent contractor transportation business, or a partnership, you will need a federal tax ID.

As a transportation company sole proprietor, you can use a federal tax ID you obtain as a business tax ID.

BUSINESS BANK ACCOUNT

This is one important step, but it can only be done after you have a fully executed article of incorporation (registered as an LLC), which has been approved by the state, and you have an EIN number assigned by the IRS.

Once you have these two documents, you should be able to go to a bank and open your first commercial bank account.

But remember to check and understand various types of commercial checking account fees, you want to find a bank that offers a free or almost free commercial checking account. Some larger banks can charge you hundreds of dollars each month, depending on how many transactions you do. Make sure to ask and shop around before you sign on the dotted line.

OBTAIN FINANCING

Money is the ultimate lifeblood of any business. Without it, you can't start or run any business. Before we get into some of the more conventional funding ideas, here are some basic ideas you should consider first.

1. Your own savings/401K, etc.
2. Bootstrap – as in, you work to pay for the startup costs
3. Home equity line of credit (this is how I got started with mine)
4. Family funding (where your parents or siblings help you with a personal loan)
5. Create a partnership with people who have the money
6. Credit cards, cash advances (Be careful with this idea)

7. Angel investors – someone always wants in on the next big thing!
8. Bank Loan
9. SBA (Small Business Administration) loan
10. Grants for small businesses

When it comes to choosing funding sources, they must match the needs of your company. You may go for the one you believe will work best for your personal situation and financial plan.

START-UP COSTS

As you talk to potential customers and refine your idea, you'll likely be getting closer to a more solid business plan, which ensures your chances of success. What you need to do next is to make sure your plan is financially viable with your current influx of money.

At this stage, you'll want to have at least a rough estimate of the minimum amount needed to start the business and a realistic expectation of whether or not you can achieve the goal.

Some costs to consider include:

Your business location. Does it cost you to have a place to store your fleet of vehicles? Are you considering renting an office space?

For the purposes of our simple startup, beginning with a senior transport service, we will run the business out of Cindy Lee's home office, which is a detached garage at her home. We can also store Susie and Cindy's cars there. Hence, this so far does not cost us anything in this scenario.

Software for scheduling and billing. The ladies in our fake business at Senior Shuttles will be using Excel to keep track of expenses and also the trip logs. For scheduling, they are initially going to use Google Calendar, which is a free online calendar tool.

As their business grows, however, they will need to invest in software. Some options they are considering are NEMT Cloud Dispatching https://www.nemtclouddispatch.com/non-emergency-medical-trans-application.html and TripSpark https://www.tripspark.com/.

Laptops for both partners. They are budgeting at least $2,000 to get two small laptops.

Utilities. They need internet access at $100/month for the business office and cell phone service with data access for two phones. They are budgeting at least $120/month for the cell phone plan.

Insurance. We will discuss the types of insurance to purchase next. The cost of this insurance varies greatly by location, company, and deductible amounts.

Vehicle costs. Here, you have to think about the costs of gas, maintenance like oil changes, buying tires, or if you want to retrofit your vehicle to be more handicap accessible.

INSURANCE

You will need adequate insurance coverage. Considering that you're transporting and interacting with people, especially the frail and elderly, you want to make sure that your business is covered in any unfortunate event.

These insurance requirements involve:

- Workers compensation

- Business personal property
- General liability
- "Full" auto insurance
- Any other unique insurance coverage

The basic requirement of any NEMT business service is for drivers to assist clients out and into the vehicle. Particularly, for new operators, some carriers perceive this insurance coverage as less desirable regarding this same level of client support.

Because of the general liability insurance and the high fixed cost of commercial auto insurance, operators can discover they are at a cutthroat detriment. Indeed, for transportation providers to consider expanding either the physical footprint of geographic areas of operation or the size of the fleet, a primary factor to consider is insurance. This means that potential customers will not understand the coverage gaps if they sustain an injury while exiting or entering the vehicle.

When transportation providers don't give a particular highlight of their coverage to their clients, the client may have nothing to claim if, while transitioning, they are hurt because the driver doesn't carry general liability insurance. This situation alone makes insurance coverage for NEMT quite tricky and expensive.

Superior coverage in insurance can be the deciding factor for setting your business apart from your competitors. It becomes unlikely that a service provider that has no focus on non-emergency medical transportation will want to call such a transportation service once they understand they may have liability.

NEMT providers can enjoy a wide range of NEMT insurance. Since several factors put NEMT companies at risk, the sense in it is that there are various aspects of NEMT insurance.

The consideration for NEMT providers ranges from third-party damage to persons and properties, bodily injuries to drivers and passengers in the case of collision, and vehicle damage, just like other transportation businesses. Another type of coverage for transportation companies is the general liability coverage as part of NEMT insurance.

Also, there are unique considerations for NEMT providers. There is a range of medical needs and expensive equipment necessary to securely and safely transport passengers, including passengers who require a wheelchair during their trip.

Another crucial aspect of NEMT insurance is the workers' compensation coverage because drivers are at a higher risk of bodily injury while helping to transport passengers. Again, it is useful to consider patients who are wheelchair users.

NEMT drivers have an increased risk of exertion-related injuries since they help to get wheelchairs into position, and doing that can put a strain on them against anything that any drivers of other transportation companies have to contend.

Private payors, Medicaid, Medicare, medical clinics, and hospitals usually compensate paratransit service companies. As a result, to protect the medical patient during transportation, there is a mandatory rule from the county and state government agencies that requires adequate insurance for NEMT businesses.

What type of insurance is necessary for medical transportation?

Some of these types of insurance include:

- Excess liability (optional)

- Commercial automobile insurance liability for the protection of your passengers in the event they get injured in your vehicle and during transportation between two locations

- Professional Liability to cover your passengers against any sexual and physical abuse caused by your employees

- For reckless driving, a passenger traveling in your vehicle can file a lawsuit against your driver, and, for necessity, general liability will cover such a trial

- In the event of an accident or theft, physical loss of your vehicles

The coverage type provided by NEMT insurance

- Passengers' loading and unloading. This type of insurance is designed for your passengers' coverage. It is under the policy of Professional Liability that this category of protection is covered, and it is necessary since, during the process of assisting passengers when exiting or entering the vehicle, your employees can cause any physical injury.

- Uninsured motorist. In a circumstance where an accident occurs involving your vehicle, this coverage compensates your passengers without the auto liability insurance of the other party.

- Non-owned auto insurance. When, on your behalf, your employee conducts business using his vehicle, this type of insurance is used for the company's coverage.

- Hired auto insurance. For you to service your business, in a circumstance where you borrowed, rented, leased, or hired a vehicle, this type is used to protect your company.

- Collision and comprehensive. In a situation of an accident or a theft, for any physical damage done to your vehicle, you get compensation through this coverage.

- Commercial auto liability. This coverage protects your company against a third-party claim. It also covers your passengers for bodily injury while riding in your vehicle.

HOW TO RUN YOUR BUSINESS

So you have the best intentions of starting and running a NEMT fleet. You have laid out the business plan, come up with a starting budget, and secured funding to get started.

But what does your day look like? What should you expect?

Let's pretend that you are Susie Quinn, and you are starting with your first day of Senior Shuttles. During the first week, you picked up the logo-branded polo shirts that you will wear with khaki pants as your uniform. You have met with and dropped off flyers and business cards to several local doctors' offices, senior care centers, and the two major hospitals in your area. This required a lot of smiles and miles to accomplish.

On your first official Monday, you get a call from your first customer! Mrs. Ledwig from Comfort Acres Retirement Park needs a ride to her podiatrist on Tuesday at 9:00 am. You get all of the details from her, including her name, address, whether she needs any ride considerations or preferences, the address of the podiatrist's office, and Mrs. Ledwig's credit card number to charge the ride. You also give her a quote based on the mileage and time spent for the ride.

As you enter the information into your software, you're excited to get your business going!

Throughout the day, you make a post to your social media accounts, retweeting a relevant news article about seniors' health.

Now your Tuesday morning is booked, considering that Mrs. Ledwig wants you to wait with her in the waiting room of the doctor's office. She also wants you to give her the return ride home.

Since you're getting your feet wet and actually providing the service you have always wished to provide, you decide that your process needs to be streamlined and organized.

CREATE A COMPANY HANDBOOK

Now is the time to write a company handbook. This should outline the processes, rules, and procedures of how your daily business operates. Some ideas for what to include in your handbook could be:

- How to handle sales calls

- What information to collect from customers

- How to state a verbal agreement for services, like a contract

- What your privacy policy is

- What are your car rules for passengers, maintenance, and drivers? Think of things like "drivers are not allowed to use a cell phone while the car is in motion," and other safety considerations.

- List of emergency procedures, including what safety items must be in the vehicle

- A grievance procedure for customers and employees

- A job description for drivers and other staff members

- Discipline procedures for employees, including common infractions like tardiness, missed rides, unkempt appearance, being rude, etc.

And anything else that makes your business tick! Think of what you would need to tell someone who was taking your place doing your job for a day. What would you need them to know?

CREATE JOB DESCRIPTIONS

So far at Senior Shuttles, it's just Susie and Cindy. But what if these ladies wanted to expand their empire? They should write specific job descriptions for staff members that they may one day have to hire.

They should start with their own job descriptions since that will most likely also be a significant component of their business plan.

Then, they could consider other staff positions, the duties of each position, and the qualities required—professional and personal—for each position.

Here is an example:

Job: Call Center Receptionist

Duties:

- Answer the phone line for every call that comes into the office
- Schedule rides over the phone

- Collect customer information while adhering to the privacy policy
- Keep track of scheduled rides, assigning drivers as needed
- Reminding drivers of scheduled rides on a daily and weekly basis

Qualifications:

One year of call center or receptionist experience.

Must have a pleasant phone voice.

Must be able to multitask.

Basic computer skills are a plus.

CUSTOMER SERVICE

At a time when businesses are learning to give priority to customer service, your company would crash and burn if it has low levels of customer service. Since a single good experience influences most consumers, one positive experience may be the factor determining their choice to stick with your brand. A negative one, on the other hand, could send them running to your competitor.

Happy Customers

By exhibiting a high standard of customer service, businesses can retain the costs of acquisition of consumers and develop a reliable consumer base that will talk about the business to family and friends. These customers could help with testimonials, case studies, and getting reviews from other customers.

When things break, and crisis happens in the company, happy customers are more understanding. They are also less sensitive when prices increase.

For this reason, investing in customer service is very important as it helps propel your business to greater levels. This is one way it helps the company.

When loyal customers are happy and receive good customer service, they spread the word about your brand to others, thus helping you acquire new customers, totally free of charge. When they spread the word, they have more potential for convincing prospective clients to your business. This makes the company more efficient than your own salespeople and marketing tools can.

In every business, retaining customers is cheaper than acquiring them.

When you increase your rate of customer retention by only 5%, you can liken that to an increase in profit of about 25%. This is because customers who keep coming back to your business are most probably going to spend more on your services. Studies show that this could go up to exactly 67% more. This later ends in your business, cutting down on the costs of operations.

When you engage in customer service, you demonstrate and build your values, mission, and, most importantly, your brand's image.

You may know and understand what your brand means and signifies. Nevertheless, your customers will not know if you do not let them know. They will interpret all that from your presence on social media, the content you give out, external marketing, and other forms of advertising.

Happy customers refer others. As mentioned earlier, when customers are happy, they are more likely to tell their coworkers, family, and friends about their good experience.

Actually, according to research by some companies, 77% of customers have told others of positive experiences with the brand. Look at it this way: if you have a fabulous experience, you are most likely to go about raving about it later that night, telling your family about the experience. It is very normal. Though unknowingly, you desire that your loved ones may commit to a brand that you trust can make them happy, too.

Word-of-mouth advertising can be the best and cheapest form of advertising. Just give your customers a reason to do it.

Good customer service encourages loyalty from customers. If a customer comes to your business and experiences something, they will have no reason to look elsewhere.

As mentioned earlier, retaining an old consumer is a lot cheaper than acquiring a new one. This essentially means that the longer a customer recurs business with you, the more revenue you can expect to generate from the single customer as a company. The longer they stay, the higher your income from them.

Building a good relationship with the customer is the key to effective customer service. Promoting a friendly, helpful, and positive environment and showing thanks to the customer will ensure that they leave the premises with a great impression.

Do not be surprised to see the happy customer returning to utilize your services.

To provide the best customer service that customers need:

- Have an idea of what your customers consider to be proper customer service.

- Take your time to research and find out what the customers expect.

- Do a follow-up on both the positive and negative responses you get from the customers.

- Make sure that you consider providing customer service in all areas of your business.

- Find ways to advance in the level of the customer service you deliver. Do this continuously, as tactics keep changing over time.

Your primary concern should be to develop a close relationship with your customers. To establish a healthy relationship with your customers, you need to:

- Approach and greet your customers in a natural way that fits that particular situation.

- Express understanding to the customer. Show them that you clearly understand their needs.

- Concentrate on people who are willing to work with you. Understand and accept that some people will not want your services.

- Offer help to people. For instance, informing a customer about a product or service that you are sure they are usually interested in is very helpful. That can take you a long way in building relationships.

- Keep reminding customers of what they are likely to gain from doing business with you.

Your clientele deserves the best experience possible from your company.

Handle Complaints Well

Every company is prone to getting complaints from customers. Pay close attention to complaints made by customers. You may discover a thing or two about your service that you had no idea about before. Inform your customers that you highly appreciate their feedback.

Refrain from making any objections, as challenging as it may be at times. Keenly listen to what the consumer is complaining about. These factors could be time or price.

Verify how valid each concern is and provide the best solution available.

HOW TO GROW YOUR BUSINESS

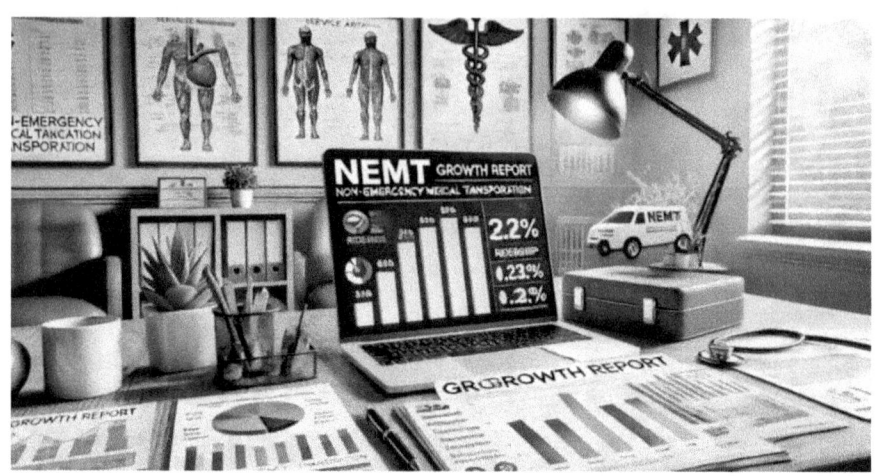

Let's revisit some ideas from when you were brainstorming about your business plan.

Advertise your transportation services to medical offices as well as assisted and retirement living facilities.

Provide presentations to local senior citizen community groups.

Sign up for a business listing with websites that help people find transportation, like Paratransit Watch.

Also, when people search for medical transportation services online, have your business appear by listing on Google Maps.

Define your sales and marketing strategies by explaining how you will find and create customers.

What are the methods your business will use to identify, attract, and convert leads? Who will handle sales, and how will you train any outside help for sales?

I would add that you should definitely form a relationship with local doctors' offices, hospitals, and other places where seniors are often found. This may require that you physically visit these places, leaving your company information in the right hands at these locations. Your friendly demeanor when introducing your business is key.

Find brokers to work with. There are Medicaid brokers and private NEMT brokers who will send sales leads your way. States are required to find a way to provide NEMT services to Medicaid recipients, so being compliant with Medicaid billing and pricing is crucial.

We will talk more about billing and insurance in the next chapter.

You can build associations with brokers, and this will help your business thrive. There are several ways to do this, but essentially, you will need to keep detailed records to meet a broker's demands. Once you can work with a broker, you will see a shift in your business, and if you can meet their demands, everyone wins.

SPREADING YOUR BRAND

After you've developed a strong brand identity, you need to spread it. To do so, you should use various marketing channels. Choose marketing that helps to connect with potential customers in person as well as online, so you can target the maximum number of people at one time.

This is essential to successful branding, and consistency is important since regular appearances of your brand will reinforce your identity and the ideal customer base. Let's look at some marketing channels you can consider.

OUTREACH

By now, you probably have a decent idea of which marketing segments to target. You need to consider your target audience and go to them, rather than waiting for them to come to you.

You want to gain a foothold in the community, and the best way to do this is through networking events and social situations where you are able to spread the word and have your business cards ready. Offering discounts is also another nice detail to add to any grand opening.

SEARCH ENGINE OPTIMIZATION (SEO)

SEO is the process of boosting your website's ranking on search engine results through keywords. This helps to grow something termed "organic" traffic, or potential leads that find your company while searching for a general product or service.

You can boost your rankings by creating intelligent and accurate information related to your service industry. This is an excellent way to boost your marketing and attract potential customers without having to pay for advertising.

SOCIAL MEDIA

Social media is a great option when it comes to putting a human face to your brand and drawing in your target audience. Consider the brand story you've been telling and develop a consistent social media voice to convey the message. Always stick to your brand story and have frequent social media engagement in order to cultivate a strong brand.

As I mentioned very briefly before, there is a growing market of older Facebook users. According to Facebook's statistics, 52% of people ages 50-64 have a Facebook account. Facebook use among people 65+ has risen 14% since 2011.

It makes the most sense for you to be where your target audience is! Create a Facebook business page for your business. This page has to be created and owned by your personal Facebook account. Once you do this, you can also connect it to your Instagram page, therefore "verifying" your business's Instagram account.

Some helpful social media tips:

- Post often, if not every single day, post every other day.

- Don't just focus on your sales and money, while advertising discounts; your followers want more than just business in that way.

- Repost and share pertinent news stories.

- Have a sense of humor! Why do you think memes are so popular?

- Think in terms of what your followers would want to see from their end, what's important to them?

- When posting a picture of your clients, make sure you have their express verbal or written permission to share their image. Be considerate of their privacy.

- Consider more than just words or still images. Utilize short videos and story formats to capture people's attention.

Billing Concerns

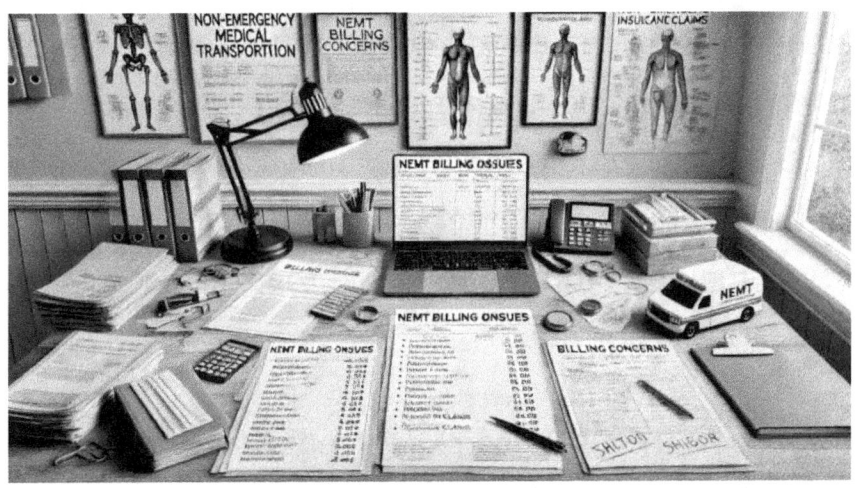

What are Medicaid's NEMT Regulations?

Since its birth, the NEMT program has been a fundamental Medicaid benefit. However, due to the Medicaid program's flexibility and the differences between states, this benefit could vary slightly.

For example, throughout the country, there are differences in the previous authorization agreements. Ahead of receiving transportation by the beneficiaries, in some states, there is a requirement for preauthorization of transportation services coverage.

The state can preauthorize transportation in several ways. For example, a physician's authorization may be part of the requirements for one state, while in another state, before offering services, the medical facility may be required to call in the request for medical transportation.

A transportation service copayment may be required. This process is usually a minimal fee that is around $0.50 and $3.50. Also, through the Medicaid 1115 waivers, there can be a limit in the NEMT programs of some states' Medicaid programs.

Since they have exhausted some payments at the end of any given month, denying a ride is not allowed for any broker by the rules. With regard to the laws of the contract, trips need to be administered by brokers. Also, contract provisions specifically outline the penalties, audits, and oversights designed to protect Medicaid members or the state, even when, for the protection of brokers, there is a provision incorporated into the contract.

Recipients of Medicaid have, by law, the right to health plan benefits. There must be a report of any scheduled trip that they missed. A payment of damage may often result if a certain percentage sums up the number of missed trips.

WHY DO THEY COVER NEMT?

A consideration that influences the health of the patient is transportation. On the wellness of the patients, supporting transportation tends to have such a profound impact because they don't have transportation to an appointment, irrespective of the status of the payer, 3.6 million people have no access to medical care, as noted in an AHA report.

As the impact of missed appointments is on the revenue cycle of healthcare, it also impacts the health of the patient. There will be a rise in the cost of healthcare due to wellness and health deterioration, which is as well as the consequence of miss appointments.

For example, with their providers, there will be a requirement to be present at their frequent check-ins for chronically ill patients. To reduce the likelihood of a costly medical event, the providers can activate essential preventive care, since ensuring the patient's condition has not deteriorated is what these appointments are meant to do. Patients are costing more healthcare money and are at risk of getting sicker when a patient finds it hard to keep up with these scheduled times.

Ways to Collect Payments

Consider hiring a medical billing service. This service can determine what copays a client is expected to pay and can also bill private insurance companies.

Take cash. This may place the driver at risk of theft since they have to carry the cash on them, but this is a viable option.

Take credit cards. This is probably the most cost-efficient route, considering that the processing company you go with will charge a transaction fee.

Take payment via an app. The most common app for payments is probably PayPal. You could research apps, similar to Uber and Lyft's rideshare apps for scheduling and payment considerations.

Consider a retainer fee or a monthly charge. If you want to retain someone's business, consider having a plan that acts as a monthly retainer fee. The customer or their beneficiary pays per month for a certain number of rides or miles in advance. Think of it as a "frequent rider" punch card, like what's used in public transit services such as subways and buses.

Encourage clients to file their own insurance claims for rides with their private insurance carrier. Place the insurance filing upon the rider by providing them with statements and receipts as necessary. Charge them your cash pay fee, just as a private payor.

CONCLUSION

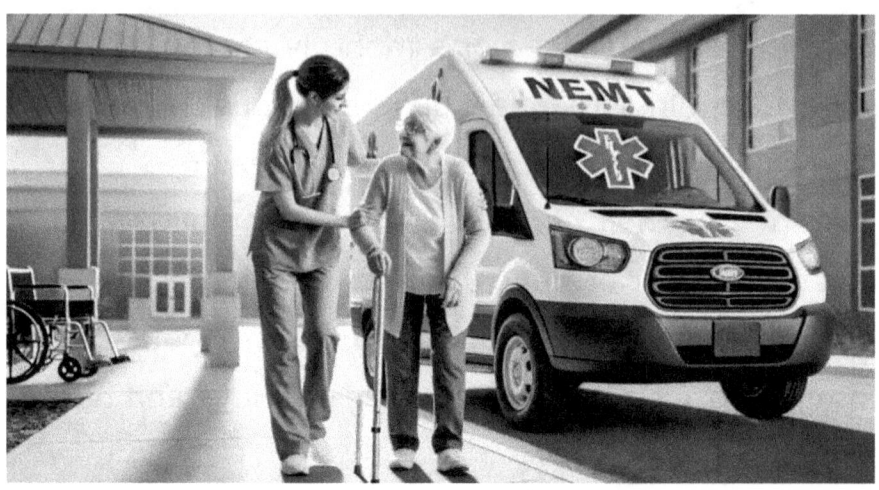

It's a cliché to say that all of our work ethics and preferences are diverse. That does not make this ideal any less factual.

The majority of American jobs force employees into a set work routine and format, which is ok for some but not for all. While some of us have always dreamed of working from home, it may not be an easy option.

What's exceptional about being a NEMT provider is that you get to help people every single day. You set your own hours, too.

If you have a family, you get to spend more time with them by working from home. If, on the other hand, you are single and like working around other people, then a shared office space might be ideal for you. You can be around people and still maintain your sanity.

Either option works fine. Try out some combination of the options available to determine what will work best for you and your business. Knowing your options for controlling your work environment makes a big difference.

In today's economy, technology tends to make work and personal time indistinguishable.

When you become a NEMT provider, being accessible to your clients is an integral part of the business. While for some markets, this high-tech imposition is a complication and a distraction, for NEMT providers, it makes achieving the essentials much easier.

For many, the most attractive aspect of being an NEMT business owner is the freedom and independence it affords.

Fortunately, it's completely doable for you to be a fully independent NEMT provider from home, but still get the help and advice you need when you encounter troubles. These issues can include late payments, hard-to-understand software, legal jargon, or claims filed against you.

This is where it becomes critical to build a strong network of supporters with experts like your attorney, long-time NEMT providers, and your friends and family.

If you combine all these teachings in this book, it's going to be quite clear to you how NEMT business owners are able to maintain their success.

At the end of the day, the key is having the resiliency to seek out what works for you and stay the course.

There is no cookie-cutter template for a successful NEMT business, and be leery of anyone trying to sell you one.

I wish you the best of luck in your future business endeavors.

If this book has helped you in any way, would you please consider leaving a review where you purchased this book? I plan on reading every review that I get so that I can improve my future writing projects.